The Hanging God

The
Hanging
God

James

Matthew

Wilson

Foreword by Dana Gioia

✢ Angelico Press

First published in the USA
by Angelico Press 2018
© James Matthew Wilson 2018
Foreword © Dana Gioia 2018

For information, address:
Angelico Press
169 Monitor St.
Brooklyn, NY 11222
angelicopress.com

Paperback: 978-1-62138-402-1
Cloth: 978-1-62138-410-6
eBook: 978-1-62138-403-8

Cover design: Michael Schrauzer
Cover image: "The Sacrifice of Odin," Lorenz Frølich
(Source: Wikimedia Commons)

In Memory of Helen Pinkerton Trimpi

We have seen reason to think that the Jewish festival of Purim is a continuation, under a changed name, of the Babylonian Sacaea, and that in celebrating it by the destruction of an effigy of Haman the modern Jews have kept up a reminiscence of the ancient custom of crucifying or hanging a man in the character of a god at the festival. . . . In this form the story of the life and death of Jesus . . . set a thousand expectant strings vibrating in unison wherever men had heard the old, old story of the dying and risen god.

                                        ~James George Frazer

CONTENTS

VI.

FOREWORD

Poetry is a language, a special way of speaking. It is not limited to a particular style or aesthetic. A language can say everything that might be said. The history of poetry is an endlessly overlapping series of conversations—between author and audience, past and present, living and dead. The medium of verse accommodates countless styles, traditions, movements and manifestations. However bewildering, that variety attests to the art's vitality.

A poet does not emerge *ex nihilo*. He or she develops out of particular traditions and affinities. Reading a new poet, especially an ambitious one, it helps to understand the writer's lineage. Out of what previous conversations does the author originate? Is the work caught up in current literary chatter or does it spring from older sources? Does the reader feel the presence of earlier writers? What perennial questions does the new writer address?

James Matthew Wilson is such a complicated, ambitious, and unusual poet that his work benefits by being put in a literary context. A generation ago it would not have been necessary to explain the tradition in which Wilson works, but *The Hanging God* stands at such distance from most popular contemporary styles that a few critical comments may be helpful.

Wilson writes in what one might call the high humanist Christian tradition. In literary terms, this is not the music of the humble shepherd's pipe but the double keyboard pipe organ—resonant, complex, and contrapuntal. This lineage represents one of the central continuities of English language poetry from Metaphysicals, such as John Donne and George Herbert, to Modernists, such as T. S. Eliot and W. H. Auden. It is not a remote historical style. Two of its masters, Richard Wilbur and Geoffrey Hill, died only in the past two years. But this once influential humanist tradition has begun to feel marginal since neither Christianity nor humanism has much appeal to today's critical establishment. For poets, however, it remains a powerful mode, though one difficult to master since it requires historical awareness, linguistic mastery, and intellectual depth. To these general demands, the poet must also bring a personal voice and individual perspective. There is no missing Wilson's deep loyalties to this tradition. His poetry is formal, classical, learned, and Catholic.

Since style is often the simplest element to recognize in an unfamiliar author, one might begin by observing Wilson's commitment to poetic form. In his verse, the language is always shaped by formal constraints, usually both rhyme and meter. While this allegiance is not so unusual in a young poet now as it might have been thirty years ago, Wilson's personal style of formalism is contrarian. He does not adopt the relaxed, populist formalism common today, which aims for a conversational texture. Wilson strives for an elevated and literary style—not so high as Hill's arch-Anglican hymnody but nonetheless subtly stylized like Wilbur's carefully shaped and pointed lyricism.

A writer chooses his or her own family. Wilson has selected some formidable ancestors, such as Robert Lowell and Richard Wilbur. Family connections, however, rarely come without family drama. Although Wilson craves the resonance of the high style, he also feels kinship with "plain style" poets such as Yvor Winters and Helen Pinkerton who prize pure diction and musical transparency. Meanwhile a grandfatherly ghost named Eliot occasionally materializes in the background. That is quite a family gathering for any young poet to control. There are moments when these literary ancestors overwhelm their putative heir, but Wilson assimilates and deploys this rich legacy with great tact. One of the many pleasures of *The Hanging God* is Wilson's dexterous modulations from verbal austerity to extravagance. The high style demands high stakes. Wilson knows when to put all his rhetorical chips on the table and when to hedge a bet.

The formal principles governing *The Hanging God* are not limited to individual poems. They appear even in the overall design of the book, which unfolds in six sections built around two long poetic sequences. One depicts a sordid and destructive love affair, the other describes the Passion of Christ. The two long poems stand in symmetrical and audaciously contrasting positions.

More contrarian still is Wilson's classicism. His is not a classicism of subject or philosophy. Rather it arises from the author's temperament. Wilson is drawn to the classical virtues of clarity, proportion, balance, and historical consciousness. Not a tepid writer, he indulges in the romantic's attraction to extreme emotions and subject matter. His instinct, however, is always to mediate, to find clarity amid the confusion. Wilson also finds a sustaining power in tradition to generate new insight and expression.

Wilson is learned and literary. In an era of what Clive James has called "Cultural Amnesia," Wilson writes from a vibrant sense of historical consciousness. Erudition has been the downfall of some poets, but Wilson manages to be learned without being obscure or condescending. His subjects are often literary, and one finds references or allusions on nearly every page, including epigraphs from Pascal, Eliot, Rilke, and Wilde as well as poems such as "Auden in China" or "The Scar of Odysseus." Wilson's literary self-consciousness expresses itself in every sentence. In keeping with the humanist mode, he places his words and images with a sense of how they have been used by earlier writers.

For many readers, however, the aesthetic elements of Wilson's style—his formalism, classicism, and sense of literary precedence—will be secondary to his Catholicism. In this agnostic age, faith is a divisive issue, especially among intellectuals. There will be no escaping the issue in reading Wilson's poetry. The Catholic worldview informs all his verse, even on secular topics. His harrowing narrative, "Wiped Out," is not a religious poem, but it is nonetheless a theological one. This short-story-in verse describes the downward spiral of depravity and despair. Catholicism is the source spring of Wilson's imagination.

There is no need to accept a Christian worldview to read Wilson's poetry. Shared ideology is not a prerequisite for imaginative literature. I would suggest, however, that a Catholic might notice different aspects of Wilson's poetry. I was especially struck by the overpowering sense of spiritual anxiety in many poems. I expected their moral alertness, sacramental sense of the world, and moments of redemptive grace. But I was startled by the dark psychological isolation they frequently portray. There is nothing sentimental and little comforting in Wilson's religious vision. In *The Hanging God*, redemption is approached through the violence and terror of Christ's Passion. If Wilson is a Catholic poet, his faith has not come without cost.

I do not mean to overpraise the volume. *The Hanging God* is not without flaws. Some poems falter. A few seem too willed, driven more by thought than feeling. But *The Hanging God* is a book that demands to be taken seriously. It will not allow casual assessment. The best poems address consequential themes with urgent emotion and intellectual authority. The collection has unusual scope and spiritual sophistication. I am thrilled to see a young writer so ambitiously strive to renovate a great tradition.

—*Dana Gioia*

I

there was once in man a true happiness of which there now remain to him only the mark and empty trace, which he in vain tries to fill from all his surroundings . . . since we have forsaken Him it is a strange thing that there is nothing in nature which has not been serviceable in taking His place; the stars, the heavens, earth, the elements, plants, cabbages, leeks, animals, insects, calves, serpents, fever, pestilence, war, famine, fires, adultery, incest. And since man has lost the true good, everything can appear equally good to him, even his own destruction

∿ Pascal

SEE

See, from the hall, the sad men sit,
  The television on, but their
Eyes turned from it,
  Left aching for an answering stare.

See, how the soft boots of this girl
  Shuffle so slowly down the stairs,
Lost in a whirl
  Of cold slights and cosmetic cares.

See, too, the light of evening rake
  The clouds that roll across the sky
And do not break,
  But silent, threatening, pass us by.

And see, and see, into the dark,
  Where spoiled wants and words ferment;
Or that strange park
  Where guilt still loiters, old and bent.

Our bodies harbor the abyss
  On whose source we all speculate:
What is its wish
  That whips our longing, goads our hate?

That leaves us glowering over its deep,
  Discerning shadow within shade,
In which we'd leap,
  If that were the sole price we paid?

Histories

Call no man happy till he is dead.
~ Herodotus

There were the winters—first, it seemed—lined up
In memory. The winters when old people
Began to die, the ones where snows disrupt
Tickets to warmer places, like a peephole
On some more sensual world, suddenly stuffed shut.
The winters when such white-outs never came
And his wife felt the fog and wind in the gut,
As harbingers that our too human game
Would sink beneath a deluge sent by God.
The January when his brother's heart
Seizured beneath the surgeon's knife; the plod
Of weeks his sister lay in bed, apart
From everyone, refused to hold her children,
And woke again, again each night to cry
That no one loved her.   But, the past was filled in
No less by seasons like a mellow sigh,
Entire days where body seemed set by,
So governed was his thought by this or that
Idea; or others, when it mounted high,
Soothed in the womblike waters, or on flat
Sands sunned to sleep.   They all resided, deep
Within the gathering archives of time's passing,
And seemed to promise fullness. Should he weep
At pain's hard calculus? Or read the amassing
Imprint of what time takes as loving gift?
He knew, in fact, from what he'd read of Solon,
He was a pulse too soon to gauge the drift
Of his still living history. He couldn't know on
What turn it'd finish; but, he saw its moving—
Even now, as he pulled the garden greens
From loose earth and breathed in their scent—its moving
Toward that last form which shows what each life means.

DURING THE PROTESTS

We praise the clink of plate on plate
Stirring in evening suds, and thank
You for the snow's refulgent weight
Which settles on the hill's high bank.

The warmth of this interior,
Its private peace, quotidian motion,
Is deepened by what lies before
Us, leavens thanks into devotion.

But on the screen stream curious scenes
Of tanks mobbed in the desert square;
We do not know what their shout means,
Their flags, their fists—far over there.

We talk of lunch and laundry, not
To plumb the pleasures of distraction,
But prudent toward an order thought
Sustaining though not satisfaction:

To train our hunger it gives rest
By freeing us of the stomach's worrying.
My wife's weight to my side is pressed
As we watch what elsewhere's occurring.

Could a day come when all is peace?
Not some mere fullness of the table
Drowsing us in each evening's ease;
Not *just* a stop to war, as stable

And preferable as that may sound.
For, far-flung chaos, present order
Must find their last food somewhere, ground
Their acts beyond the bluest border.

It's for that land we praise you; know
The taste of it within our mouth;
The figure of it in the snow;
And, in that desert rage, its drought.

To Ernest Hilbert

Somewhere between John Lennon's name as pop
    Icon and as the spirit of an age,
    Where the tradition goes upon eviction,
Extends an alley littered with its crop
    Of foam cups, cigar butts, champagne, a page
    From William James, *GQ*, or *True Crime* fiction.
This poor, neglected corridor divides
    The office suites a rare books dealer rents
    From kitchen noises at a grand hotel
Where cakes are being iced for naïve brides.
    It echoes a street prophet's loud two cents
    That nothing without whiskey can end well.
How you found this place, Ernie, I don't know,
    But in your books, you hold it up for show.

RECKONINGS

With fingers tensed and curled, my brother wheeled
    Us down the level highway, toward Celina.
To every side, the eye met field on field

Of soy, the little stems primped tight with leaf,
    And tapering to a halt at the horizon's
Picket of ashes. He asked in his brief

And diffident way what I was studying
    These days, and jabbed a thumb at the back seat,
Where my pack slouched, unzipped, with books. A string

Of sentences, of nouns lost in their floating,
    Drifted and drowned. My eyes tight on the road,
My legs clenched, and my brother quiet, noting

Each flail and stab at speech. I should have known
    He'd ask, of course, and wanted him to ask,
A bold breath ready. But no, I was thrown

Off, all thought choked and dying in my throat.
    So have I been caught out in other ways,
Left stuttering what I should have voiced by rote

In every moment whose eye—more mature
    Than mine, and practical—asks, "Who are you?
And what?" then stares the road down straight and sure.

THE RECLUSE
Mishawaka

From a bowed plastic chair and balcony,
　Three stories up, the sun a burning plate,
Rain gutters thick with blackened leaves, I see
　The trailer park, the toll road, and a great
Brown dumpster bear their burdens placidly.

But I cannot—refuse to—and I sit,
　A blank stare for those passing in the street,
And none for news come in the mail, for it
　Is graver than the looks my neighbors greet
Me with, which seem a blend of bile and spit.

It's broken me so I can barely stand.
　I've heard rejecting laughter, forced to live
Where bodies turn on reflex just to strand
　The man whose face shows he has nil to give,
Felt clear contempt as someone shook my hand.

In other times, men crushed by sneers or scorn,
　Would, with a decent wisdom, beat retreat
From public pain to where it might be borne.
　Such men stood silent on unmoving feet.
So I sit, sore, apart, as the great horn
　　Of factories letting out, the highway's blare,
　　All chorus, mocking, "Who said life was fair?"

In Sickness

Our first kiss, I remember, came
As you showed off a brand new dress,
While I laughed at your pouty claim
You'd die some lonesome anchoress.

The world is packed with the unwed
And gorgeous falling on their swords,
The young impassioned, who have said
That fate will send them heavenwards

Before they feel one sincere kiss
Or know attention that is more
Than clammy-hand flirtation. This
Was not my plan. I meant much more.

But, have you seen how the sun's rays
A moment leave the clouds enflamed?
This night, in thought, that lost night plays—
That kiss of which I've grown ashamed.

I serve you tea and aspirin,
Your body sweating, fevered, chill.
I wait for you to heal, and, when
You have—I'll leave for good. I will.

For if our love sprang from my terse
Laugh and peremptory kiss, its going
Will come more soft and be the nurse
Of an indifference just now showing.

AGRICOLA: A SONG FOR PLANTING

My arms have labored such small cares
And failed them. So little as one seed,
I've sown or tossed among the tares,
Shriveled with thirst and failed to feed.

I've looked with hope on stony ground.
I've scythed the grain at autumn's blush.
But now, the earth is cold; the browned
And fallen husks of last year crush

Beneath my booted step. This year
Threatens to end new growth in drought;
These dead stalks tokens of that fear
For what our efforts bring about.

What pretty lie did I speak when
I cast my efforts to sustain
Each growth? Each year forgives my sin,
But remnants of each loss remain.

The Consolation of Oranges

As I sat quietly thinking about my death and venting
my anguish in verse, I sensed a woman standing at my
shoulder. Her brilliant appearance struck me with awe,
her eyes burning with an unnatural heat. She was so
ancient that I could hardly confuse her with the women
of my age. . . . Her gown was woven of some enduring
metal thread . . . nonetheless torn by the ravishing of
savages, who had carried off whatever they could. In her
right hand, some books; in her left, a scepter.
                                              ∽ Boethius

I

This happening just off the trail
Along the Quabbin Reservoir:
She whispers, bruised hand taking hold
Of my arm, her face drawing close,

Though no one for at least two miles.
It was, in fact, that emptiness
I'd been referring to in pointing
To a lone pine, shivering among

A naked stand of wiry birches,
The scar of ashen trunks, the dead
And shaking limbs against the sky.
"A symbol of some sort," I said.

She answered, "Atheists are those
Who, having looked at symbols spelled
In branching letters, scattered dust,
See only things, not what they mean."

II

The sun rose to reveal her at her station,
Where I dreamed she had come in consolation

Bringing wise thought, sweet words, a book in hand.
But somewhere past, she'd touched me as I scanned

For stones to skip across the purpled water,
Held back my arm, said she was Zion's daughter.

9

"No," I said, "we are just out for a walk."
"But not that only." She began to talk.

III

My feet turned on the steps, worn smooth
As river stones, in the high stairwell.
The first white flecks of blood orange peel
I hardly noticed, where they lay

Torn and stripped by a fingernail.
But one floor up, a longer band,
More generous, a sphere filleted
And flattened as cartographers

Mash an idea of the earth
On paper. Farther on, last bits
Of rind, dimpled and white, gleamed up
Like promises of coming sweetness.

I reached the intended corridor,
And there found, dropped and kicked aside,
The slouched, uneaten muscle of
The broken body of the orange.

IV

It was as if I'd followed him.
Some boy, whose stub nail dug it free,
Following his mother upward, toward
The waiting room for cancer patients,

His backpack full of picture books.
She'd made the first incisions with
A painted nail and left to him
The prying back of willing skin,

Scenting the stairwell's empty air.
But no slick jewel of pulp plumped out.
His disappointment, then, to turn,
As, "Here," she says, "Hurry," she says,

He starts to free a gelid segment.
But in the unfamiliar light,
The heavy door she holds for him,
The sound of someone's steps below,

Fast winding up that peel of stairs—
Not even a taste between his teeth—
He sees it drop against the mopped,
Much-traveled landing at his feet.

V

This comes not as a thought of mine,
But as if an interior part
Of that distended corpse of fruit.
Forget the stripped and creaking boughs

That bend beneath the mind's cold wind.
If she were here, she'd ask me, who
Could climb that stair the hue of mud,
Who see the freckled stuff of life

And human hands and not find signs
Leading to bright and resonant stores?
"You'll find those stories carry stories,"
She'd say, to show words tucked in things,

Much like the child in Mary's womb,
Or Boethius' words dreamed as a woman.
Even before that final sight,
The orange skin gave more of itself,

Hinting at form like a world that
Keeps rolling up from in its map,
Like trees whose narrow trunks conceal
Some living sap of mystery.

So, also, from that darkening bruise,
Between her thumb and forefinger
Where some nurse had put in the needle,
I knew that it was her as well,

Turning above me on the stair.
I would have been that little boy,
I would have dropped my food to follow,
But no thought of mine could catch me up.

She was the girl who sounded bright.
She was the one who spoke in dreams,
She was the one who closed the door
And found herself there all alone.

II
THE MOUNTAINS OF CHINA

AUDEN IN CHINA

In January Nineteen-Thirty-Eight,
He sailed for China, hired to report
On the rough seams of tank treads in the mud,
The peaks of blue paint shrouded with gray mist,
And the wall, ancient, incomplete, inhuman.
Its tumbling blocks and snake-wind toward the sea
Reminded him of how a land endures
The free-willed drift of history, and how
The remnant of past enemies, the floods
That rise, consume, recede, remain like scars,
Or stain to mossy lime a russet stone.
    What had been practical now rests athwart
A landscape burned beneath a rising sun:
"They carry terror with them like a purse...
And cling and huddle in the new disaster."
    He watched the refugees flee in a tongue
As meaningless to him as was that wall
To the invading Japanese, and toured
Through emptied villages. He squinted at
The lights of decorous diplomacy,
Where jazz collided with the lanterned dark,
And bobbed hair squared the faces of rich women.
Both they and he were "wandering lost upon
The mountains of our choice..." Both they and he
Must "live in freedom by necessity,
A mountain people dwelling in the mountains."
    But when his tripper's task was done, and pens
Packed in a row like ammunition, he
Alone would turn to meet the landless freedom,
Where not a precipice survives its forming,
The moment's surge of foam and wave against
A steel bow. China, Spain, and Ethiopia
Sinking in war, all piled stones returning
To scattered atoms, wave beneath black wave.
He stared into the "changed and shaken" sea,
That lonesome interlude of liberty.

An Interlude

Beside the bronze flow of a river,
By mud slicked reeds and willow trees
Whose every leaf hangs like a sliver,
A girl of high birth bathes skinned knees.

Youth still shines out of her as light
Beams through the cut glass of a door
And brightens a small patch of night.
Some innocence or pride in store

Blushes the bruised curve of her cheek.
And she—as though she senses it,
Yet never could find words to speak
Of hard forced kisses, or the spit

And kicks that trailed her down the stairs—
She lifts gnawed fingers to her face
To brush away some wind-blown hairs,
And there now hardness shadows grace.

Not long ago, she was a whore.
And now she is a drunkard's wife.
He doesn't come home anymore,
Her bed cold as a waiting knife.

BEI DAO IN YPSILANTI

The slopped white paint on echoing cinder blocks
And Tourette's-tic from high-set ceiling lights
Gave to the sparse-filled lecture hall the same
Tyrannical efficiency he'd found
In every revolutionary plan.
As he strolled down its sloping aisles, he seemed
To hear a guard's stout warning and begin
Years of imprisonment with neither trial
Nor hope that even a single word, one's name,
Might penetrate the bleaching bricks: "The honest
Man bears his honor like an epitaph."
    Perched on the lectern's rickety bulk, Bei Dao
Twanged alien syllables in quick staccato.
I waited, with the old enthusiasts,
The working mother back for her degree,
And half-stoned undergraduates, for the plump
American professor to step forward
And sift to English all those wiry chords:
"If sea should break the sea wall down, then let
Its brackish water fill my heart, if the
Land rise up from the sea again, we'll choose
Again to live upon the heights . . . those ancient
Ideograms, the future's eyes, gaze back."
    Such were the words reported to us, such
As came by the exile's throat from some time
In the imprisoned past. How thin and dark
He seemed against the stage's bright orange curtain.
I thought how strange that this should be a place
For waiting out a government's ill will:
Sheltering near the carcass of Detroit,
Its burnt-out rows of houses ruled by dogs,
Abandoned, mauled, with missing eyes and paws.
Where glaciers many thousand years before
Had leveled out the mountains and the sea,
He spent his days as one more teacher in
An edifice of mass re-education:
His lonesome voice was safe to shape its words,
Where, with a smattering of applause, the world
Would carry on indifferent and unravelling.

The Wild Geese

A stolen horse will never pasture well
And flocks of white-downed birds prefer to keep
A strict path, looped from north to south, avoiding
The frozen miles beneath. We dwell on plains
Of habit, and become the necessary
Colonists of routine.
                              How many croppies
Fled execution, chose exile instead,
And service in Napoleon's ranks?
                                        One stood,
Staring at the smoke rising from Smolensk,
The burned and frozen path beyond that lead
To all the dead at Borodino, Moscow,
Emptied of all save a few cats and convicts.
Snow fell, then spiraled back into the sky.
He felt lice creep beneath his collar and
Against his neck, and felt himself half-driven
Under a standard red and blue, and driven
Forward without hope of return. Each round
He fires, every soldier left recumbent
In blood, goes paid but unrewarded. It
Has been ten years since he last stood in Wexford,
But can imagine his gray head—bruised, severed,
And set up on a wavering pike as warning—
Among those lions who died across the sea.

Sean Golden in Sligo

(refrains from Gu Cheng)

I met his darkened eyes long after they
Had given up their search for light. Behind
Thin circle lenses he stared out at me,
Holding a full black pint close to his chest,
The thump of bodhran and a keening girl
About us in the thick packed pub. *The ship
You've boarded's fate lies under the red sea.*

For years he had taught English at the school
Where I now studied. I had heard of him.
Belated victim of the Cold War, he
Was fired, they said, because he had taught Marx,
Russian and Chinese politics, when they'd
Hired him to cover Irish poetry.
*Each day you went the way you should go, toward
An unknown sea of unsure tides.*

                      No work,
No family, no country even, cast out
From the rhetorical world of academe,
He thought to send his body where his mind
Imagined it had been for years: to China.
He picked up Mandarin and lived among
Survivors of the Cultural Revolution.
He saw how children in the most remote
Villages were as healthy and well fed
As those in Beijing. Even birth defects
Were not ignored. And yet, he also saw
A state impatient with its old ideas
And restless with its cash.

                       Again, he wandered,
Now teaching Chinese literature wherever
A chance job came. Whenever he thought of China,
He now thought of a land that hope had fled
And set itself *to wander on the peaks,
Dreaming another land, another world.*
Her great mass flooded, left, with no desire
But for new movies, cars, and factories,
And to leave children in their villages,
Burnt faces cleft by harelips, fingers veined
And stretching toward the smoke and steel of Beijing.

III
WIPED OUT

The true mystery of the world is the visible, not
the invisible.

～ Oscar Wilde

I

She was a liar—pathological,
    I mean—and so, when we had our last fight
    And she left screaming, it was logical
    To trash the photos of our trashed delight—
All cuddle-headed, grinning in the light
    Of barroom neon signs, our faces rising
    Above the glassy necks of bottles—, right?
    Delete her number, cut her friends, reprising
All she had purred in bed as fantasizing.
    Why wear the tattoos of an episode
    Of which the facts, in fact, were mere disguising,
    Signified nothing, or less than they showed?
But those hot pleasures I took on her flesh
    Couldn't be forgot or—better—had afresh.

II

She said she was in nursing school: a lie.
    A lie, that she had moved to town to care
    For her frail grandmother—whom she'd watched die.
    Her grandpa had been a preacher. Knelt in prayer,
She sometimes heard his voice; it was a scare,
    Or so she said, but it was all untrue.
    The night we met, she wore no underwear,
    And when my hand slipped up her leg, I knew
The moist heat waiting where thighs part. "Do you
    Believe a man and woman should be married
    Before they make love? *I* do—*think* I do,"
    She whispered, warm lips to my ear. I carried
Her to her room, hearing the tentative tone.
    A whopper: I was the first to make her moan.

III

I got what her eyes promised, that's for sure,
    And usually several times a night. As she
    Straddled my hips and arched, I felt as pure
    As any knight who'd raise, in charity,
An orphaned student nurse from poverty.
    When I found condom wrappers in the chest
    Beside her bed, when we met—constantly—
    Frat boys who bought her shots and eyed her chest
As if they were confused to see it dressed,
    My ears would drink in every lame excuse:
    The rubbers, her old roommate's; she confessed
    The boys were family friends she couldn't lose,
Having lost *so* much in her life already.
    Not me, I'd mouth. Oh, no, I'm true and steady.

IV

A stripper, that's what she turned out to be,
   Working the rusted holes of the Midwest,
   Its sullen dives with deadbeats drunk by three,
   Its bouncers with shaved head and swarthy chest
Who'd guard their pride with claims to be the best
   At *something* we could never see them do.
   Hungry to get her home, I came to rest
   Among them, nursing beers, a shot or two.
Her lies were like a ditch I'd veered into:
   "She's just a huge-racked innocent," I'd *thought,*
   Brazilian wax and all, and we would screw
   Just once. But she rode me till I was caught,
And, then, one night, said "dance" was what she did.
   I did not stop. I did not even skid.

V

You hear sometimes the things a guy's believed,
    And search his eyes to check if he is joking,
    But find a glassy earnestness, deceived,
    No doubt, but real. And when you blow a smoke ring
To sign indifference, it just ends up coaxing
    More out of him: how he was celibate
    Until he met her; how, when she lies stroking
    The coarse hairs at his waist, he cannot wait
To buy what ring he can and set a date.
    If she would just say yes, he says, he's sure
    She'd quit her frequent weekends out of state
    With old friends. "Wait," you start, "What's with the *tour*?"
So would I ask myself, half conscious of
    The lust and lies from which I'd built my love.

VI

A man grows used to anything, we say,
    And makes the best of what small world he knows.
    So, sunk in smoke and disco lights that'd play
    Upon chalked nipples, thighs that hide, expose,
Until the girls' round humps slid from their clothes,
    I tried becoming friends with old, bald Jack.
    He sipped beer from an engraved mug, would pose
    For photos with the dancers, and had a knack
For pasting wholesome words on sordid flack.
    So all the girls were "actresses" with "sass,"
    A D.J. with a studded nose and track
    Marks down his arm was "Gentleman, first class."
He'd brush their cleavage with his white mustache,
    While fingering in their G-strings crumpled cash.

VII

Most nights, if she was dancing, I would sit
   On a stool near the regulars, and we
   Would buy rounds, talk of work or boats. I fit
   Right in, it seemed, though they'd stare skeptically,
When she'd come from back stage to visit me
   During her breaks, her hair slick from the shower
   And body in some felt gym suit you could see
   Was damp and hugged her breasts with a strange power.
Then, one night, at the usual closing hour,
   When we would down a shot, then head on home,
   She struts in heels right by me as I glower,
   And drives off with some jerk with teeth like chrome.
I tried to chase. My new friends blocked the door.
   And one, when I fought, threw me to the floor.

VIII

Was this a dream? I'd find myself, at night,
    Slouched in the driver's seat outside her place,
    Waiting where I could see the bedroom light,
    Should it come on, or catch her in a race
To the front door, with time to grab her face,
    Whether to kiss or smash it I couldn't tell.
    I kept myself drunk; memory'd interlace
    With need and hate, until my groin would swell.
Some nights, I'd stagger up to press her bell,
    Though I knew that she had been gone for days,
    And the dim glass became a kind of hell
    That fixed me till the sunrise made it blaze.
One night, she called my cell, asked where I'd been,
    And stood, aroused and bare, as I came in.

IX

Remember. In the greasy vinyl booth,
 We'd split a late-night breakfast. Under bare
 Fluorescent lights, I'd wallow in the smooth
 Cream of her skin, the gold coils of her hair.
The things she'd say, as if she didn't care
 If she were laughed at, came out like a mystery
 That grew still deeper with each thought she'd share,
 And even her lies now drew me to her history.
That was the point, I see now. All the glistery
 Surfaces she'd show off and then conceal
 Gave to both word and flesh their opaque witchery
 Where they were all the secret they'd reveal.
How often in bed, what I took for confession
 Was just the stock-in-trade of her profession.

X

Sometimes, I'd try to read, or sit through Mass,
   Wanting to exorcise her from my head,
   And would: a minute or an hour'd pass
   Without the thought of her lain with legs spread.
And, sometimes, we met in a hotel bed
   To swarm each other's bodies, and then sleep,
   For all we had to say had now been said,
   And in between us boredom'd quietly seep.
To break it, she'd storm out, or start to weep
   At some new lie, then blubber that she loved me.
   It came so easy to her it felt cheap,
   And even her orgiastic cries above me
Seemed now the nervous reflex of a body
   That'd stripped itself of all that wasn't body.

XI

Just when I thought that I'd been left alone,
    No longer stalked by want and jealousy
    While watching men watch *her* flash the unknown
    On stage, left with cold hours previously
Warmed by her honeyed breasts that came to me
    Ripe for the touch from hours of others' eyes
    Stroking them in a barstool fantasy,
    My telephone rang. It was some throaty guy's
Low voice, "I hear you've got a jumbo size."
    The next night, someone called again, again
    Asked was I "horny." At first, my replies
    Were to hang up or slur something profane.
But as the nights dripped on, when a ring came,
    I'd wait to hear some stranger speak my name.

XII

I listened to the callers' breath, the dark
    Out of which shot taunt and solicitation.
    One might ask if I'd meet him in a park
    To bare my loneliness for his predation,
While others, if it were some aberration—
    "You queer?"—that spurred the girls to cast me off.
    Drunk, maybe bored, they'd found the same notation
    Scrawled by the stale slates of some men's room trough.
"I'll just keep talking till I've heard enough
    To find out where they got my name and number,"
    I'd tell myself, then hear a darker laugh,
    Not the phone, but a hole that would not slumber
In me that only her live shape could fill,
    But which I, restless, stuffed and tried to still.

XIII

The bartender stood playing with her black
    Hair, combing it down one tan tattooed shoulder.
    Too early yet for college kids to pack
    The smoky booths and beer-soaked rugs, some older
Drunks nursed the happy hour specials. When I told her
    Why I'd come, she just held a Sharpie out,
    And said, "The men's room's by the smokes," not colder
    But less surprised than you would think. The grout
And tiles were flecked like the scales on a trout
    Starved in a murky tank, and, on the wall,
    In black, my name and failings all spelled out.
    I scored the marker through her words, so all
Was wiped out with my strokes. When it was done,
    Our lines were sealed in that dark block as one.

XIV

It will not wash away: all that would flick
    The fine mesh of the nerves or lured my eye
    As if it were a tongue to lick and lick
    Her tits, the sleek recess where thigh meets thigh.
Left blinking at her absence, I will try
    To think, "If I'd done this…" or "If she'd just…"
    As if this were a story, not a lie,
    In which some chaptered logic tells what must
Or must not come to pass. The law of lust
    Knows nothing of all this; says that the shape
    Our lives may seem to take is blown to dust
    At the hot breath of chance upon our nape.
All knowledge, judgment burn within its fire;
    It leaves us just the hard stone of desire.

IV

What is a person without this? What is a person without a life-form, that is to say, without a form which he has chosen for his life, a form into which and through which to pour out his life, so that his life becomes the soul of the form and the form becomes the expression of his soul?

∼ Hans Urs von Balthasar

Passover

A woman sitting in a restaurant,
Over a plate of rice and Chinese pork,
Holds back her hair with one hand, with the other
Presses flat the cheap paperback she's reading.
I see her there and think about those times
I've sat in hotel lounges with a beer
And waited for someone to ask about
The weather. But, it's early in the evening.
The bar staff's busy cutting fruit and stocking
Their knee-high fridges tight with jilting bottles.
They glance at me a couple times, as if
Confused that I'd disrupt their focused quiet
Before real customers drown out the muzak.

A few years back, my chimney started smoking.
This was just after Christmas, or, now that
I think about it, maybe just before.
I called a sweep, and from the second he
Got his black sheets spread round the hearth and set
His tools up in an expert semicircle,
He never once—not once, I'm sure—stopped talking.

At first, he wanted to describe the genius
Of damper, heat shield, chimney: to extol
The virtues of some mason long ago
Who could not hear us but had done good work.
And then, by turns, he started talking of
The miracles of the Old Testament,
The cross-shaped splattering of blood the Jews
In Egypt brushed upon their doors, one night,
To signal that the angels bringing death
Should pass them by. I saw the other children
Lying in their cribs with fingers curled toward heaven
Or what had snatched their breath. Was he a scout
Or something from some tin shack Bible Church,
Set where the hills go flat, where split-railed horse farms
Give way to sodden fields and trailer parks?

He was, or had been, so he said, at last,
A junior champ in some state scripture quiz.
I signed a check and showed him to the door.

We wait and wait, as if it were a kind of digging

Through ashes for a buried, burning ember.
We press the spines of books until they crack,
And when we've seen their stories to the end,
We do not know what we're to do with them,
As if they're strangers stopped at the wrong house.

THE SCAR OF ODYSSEUS

In the old stories, on a quest
For a lost grail, gold fleece, or to refound
A kingdom sacked that the hearth gods may rest,
    A small crew leaves its natal ground
And sails beyond the limits of the West.

    The sons and wives who stayed behind
Would wonder at their wandering and wait
With thoughts of monsters weighing on their mind,
    Until a ship with magical freight
Appears with white sail on the sea's dark rind.

    Such tales can hardly fail to please.
For, we lap up the unknown that's made known,
And sense our lives, in great or small degrees,
    Look like quests too—could they be shown
In all their menaces and victories.

    No wonder, then, we celebrate
The bliss of bride and groom at their beginning;
The perilous hours that thread a narrow strait,
    But somehow keep the fates' spool spinning;
The disembarking for a golden estate.

    What's more, we see a dark plot swells
Along the path the schoolboy walks alone;
And hear behind the girl's first kiss church bells;
    And feel our hearts with his atone,
When the bond clerk comes clean on what he sells.

    Their lives show ours. When we behold
Some soldier stiffly called away to war,
Or hear monks pray their office in the cold
    Chapel, we know that their forms are
Those our lives take when their true depths are told.

    But they must *not* be: we have seen
The maniac proclaim his destiny,

And suffered through dull cruise slides, scene on scene,
    As some fool reeled in vanity.
We cannot always say what our lives mean.

    Not just the humble, but the wise,
Accept the distant idyll for its feignedness,
Which gives to our lives' plots their just disguise.
    Odysseus wore a beggar's plainness
So that the truth his love alone'd surmise.

BRIGHT APPLES

On this particular morning, the garage
Had donuts set out near the urn of coffee;
Brought by the boss, the secretary told me,
From an old cider mill on the west edge
Of Chester County. She had more to say,
About his generosity and how
I ought to take my children—if I had them—
Out there, when autumn came. The leaves would turn
And golden red would come to apple flesh
And drive their ripe weight down into the clay.
The deer would come as well, to crop the fruit,
Fattening themselves against the snow's long burial.
It seemed like a descent into nostalgia
To think of this, so hot the summer was,
As if the future were all burning pavement.
    The heavy woman sitting next to me
Had one thick leg propped out—a broken femur,
She said, and rubbed her cane against the black
Boot she still wore, because it hadn't healed
All these months on. I tried to show my sympathy
With a grave nod, but that was not enough
For her. She levered on her stilt, then shuffled
Up to the secretary at her desk.
Settling her weight upon the cane's head, she
Explained that with the injury she'd lost
Her job, and now was caring for her mother,
Whose emphysema meant she had to stay
In bed, hooked up to oxygen. Near the end,
I guessed, and stared down at my open book.
    They were descendants of George Washington,
The woman added, as if to explain
To the still-smiling secretary and
Anyone who would hear—which in effect
Meant me—how far they'd fallen in their sorrows.
Now, here she was, her Chrysler on the rack,
Waiting all morning just to hear what's wrong.
    "They'll let you know just soon as they find out,"
Promised the secretary, and I wondered,
Did she believe the stories people told her

Or smile through them till she punched the clock,
The words of strangers, children, donuts, all
So many little details falling and gone.
   The air was streaked with heat against the glassy
Front of the shop, gleaming in summer's climax.
From a blue door, propped open near the back,
Came the ring of a wrench being let to drop
Against the concrete floor, and a hydraulic
Lift humming as its load at last descended.

Dreams That Come Friday

Take this man, golf shirt soiled with sweated stains,
Wondering at the net worth of his pains,
To balance, as it were, his coffee-brewer
Reprieve from hernia and hairs grown fewer, fewer.
Dreams of retirement his sole consolation,
Though HR reps. advise against elation.
He tallies on Excel the wealth of other
Men, thinking he might someday be their brother
Instead of glabrous Richard from Accounts,
Once they see how much his work ethic counts.
Then, affluence will ride in on the crest
Of a gold wave that breaks against his chest,
Breaks the way poets claim they feel the muse
Plucking their heart strings with ethereal news.
The difference is that poets write the note,
While he just wishes that he owned a boat.
    Wan dreams of Jimmy Buffet and white sails,
The promise of his private heaven, fails
To come to anything but charts in black
And severe stiffness of the lower back.
He scratches figures on a yellow pad,
Each stroke a quick subtraction of time had,
Now spent. These aren't the numbers of his dream,
But just the quarterly reports they seem.
"I have my aspirations, that is fine.
If I must serve the corporate design
To make myself someday incredibly rich,
That's also fine; unless you know a witch
Who'd rather grant a wish than cast a spell
For one who wants just to retire well."
    The burned dirt taste of coffee in his mouth
Blows gusts through all these dreams of sailing south,
Returns him to his proper task: "That's what
I'm paid to do," he smiles, then turns to shut
His basement office shades so that the feet
Of passersby in rain-proofed shoes won't greet
His creased but docile eye. "I'll leave at eight,"
He says, "but, please, now, please, brain, concentrate."

The picture of this man is neither cruel
Nor fanciful. He'll join the office pool
For charity, in hopes he'll win a cruise.
He'll try to cheat—invariably lose.
You might try saying this: "His dream is noble.
Such fancies help the humble think they're mobile."
I dare you. Or try out: "A pity this,
Living on borrowed, banal images
That crowd out memories of lost innocence
Which might have served him in his soul's defense."
Personally, from time to time, I come to hate him,
Because he thinks someday his boss will rate him
A peer for having been a good subordinate.
The job gets done; they don't care if he's *bored* in it.
But judgment has no sure place in these rhymes;
As someone said, the men are as the times,
And he more so than most. Where should I stand,
What must I come at last to understand,
If I would weep or smile, the Friday he gets canned?

They were at dinner. "Is that how you met Dave?"
She asked. "I mean, some group for recently
Divorced and lonely men?" "No, after that,
Way later," Bresson said; "He had moved on.
In fact, the way he talked, you'd think he was
One of those bachelor types who hop from girl
To girl with no excuse besides the season's
Changed." "Gross," she said, and took a drink, then dabbed
Her lips with the cloth napkin, smoothed it out,
And spread it once again upon her lap.
   He'd noticed when she came in how her hips
Pressed tight against her skirt; her legs were lean
And pale and made him think of the word "flesh."
And now, he thought, she's interested: she knows
The wine might stain her teeth.
                She smiled, then said,
"If you'd known him before, his wife, Michelle,
You wouldn't believe it—how he's changed, how he
Could put so much into someone, and now…"
   "Now, not," he said.
              "When things were near the end,
He'd brought in some new client: I won't say
The name. You'd know it. Big. And, well, Michelle
Comes home from work to find him dancing, like,
Just dancing—you know, right out on the driveway,
His shirt flaps hanging out, his collar open.
She'd always known he loved her—so devoted,
I mean, she'd almost stayed with him because
She couldn't understand it and felt bad
She couldn't give it back." Bresson jumped in,
"Now, not," he said again, "not him."
                 "He looked,
Prancing out in the drive, not loving but
Pathetic. Three weeks later, she moved out,
Left him the house. She couldn't *look* at him."
   He'd booked the table, and the movie she
Had picked up tickets for would start at ten.
Plenty of time to linger and fill in
The privacy that dining couples lent

With just that sort of talk one wouldn't risk
On a first date—not normally, at least,
But *maybe* if it had been set up by
One's balding colleague, the roving divorcé.
    Bresson had heard the show was straight up gore,
Two hours of blood and screaming; she insisted
Reviewers called it brooding and suspenseful.
But either way, between that odd choice and
The second bottle of the Chateauneuf
Du Pape he'd ordered when she didn't shake
Her head immediately, it seemed to him
That either they were comfortable together
Because they were *together* (and so, Dave,
Whom Bresson knew just from the club, and whose
Life seemed a wild, not-quite-sordid, string
Of stories about women, had been right),
Or just because, when the film ended, they
Would never be again. He filled her glass.
    The salad on his plate was mostly gone,
A few dark sprigs, brown beads of vinegar
Stranded in oil. Beyond its glassy front,
He saw the restaurant's lights, gleaming on slick
Macadam, and the traffic headed south,
Slowed by the rain, with wipers beating, furiously.
    "One time I went out with his ex. Michelle,
I mean. They'd settled the divorce, and she
Was trying to hold onto as many friendships
As possible. Most people blamed her, then;
And, well, okay, I thought, if he's pathetic,
You had to know that going in. To me
He seemed a little awkward, that was all.
He told dumb jokes, but I don't know a single
Guy in our office who could tell a good one."
Bresson sat mute, unwilling to prove her point.
    "In any case, she tells me, one night, after
The separation, she'd come home—I guess
Real late. Perhaps she'd been out with a man.
She didn't say. I mean, she didn't want to.
She took her dress off, left it on the floor,
And went to wash her face. She might've been
In there five minutes. When she comes back out—

My God—she finds him standing there, right in
Her bedroom, holding that red dress, it all
Throttled and twisted, wrapped around his fists.
He looked at her awhile, and that was it."

"He *left*, you mean?"

"She said it looked as if
He wanted just to do or tell her something,
Anything—you know—as if to show he could."

V

THE STATIONS OF THE CROSS

We all are falling.

~ Rainer Maria Rilke

I. Jesus Is Condemned

I tried to think for half an hour
About the face of earthly power
   That would condemn a god to die.

I listened for its menacing cackles,
The crack of whips, the clank of shackles,
   And searched for dark flames in the eye.

Through the church window I heard shrieks
Of ambulances whose techniques
   Would help us to forget our wound;

The certain hum of homeward motors,
A candidate's rank appeal to voters,
   In these its stare and voice I found.

For we sit kind, when comfort's here,
But draw our weapons with our fear
   Should someone our least want deny.

II. Jesus Takes His Cross

In every lifting of a phone
To a hot ear; in every moan
   Rising from a disheveled bed,

In each unfolding of the paper
To check his shares or learn who raped her;
   In overhearing what lawyers said

Traveling between rail stations: our
Bodies strain for the weight you bore.
   Oh, we would be weighed down instead.

III. Jesus Falls the First Time

There is a question scholars ask,
Or used to ask: given the cask
    Of vital spirits that was Christ's tomb,

Can our age speak of tragedy
Anymore? Or is comedy
    The only plot left in the room?

Where Hector glowered at his shield,
Knowing that fate would never yield
    Till ruin spread over the place he stood,

Now, the scene that follows a fall
Is an uplifting, after all:
    Lazarus comes out and eats some food.

I'm sure you wondered much the same,
As your back opened up in pain
    And sprawled beneath the blood-soaked wood.

IV. Jesus Meets His Mother

Her face seems calm, when he descries her
Dark mantle, and sees that her eyes are
    Counting the strokes scored on his back,

Noting where woven thorns imprinted
Kingship on his brow, how rust-tinted
    With damp the dust runs in his track.

He feels her kiss against his shut eye,
And tries to tell her he will *not* die.
    She says she'll see him through the race.

After all, she's heard every word;
Her heart received them undisturbed,
    And undisturbed, now, her soft face.

But, the authorities speak with one accord:
That heart's pierced seven times by a sword,
    And bleeds for being so full of grace.

V. Simon Helps to Carry Jesus' Cross

He had a bit of coin for funning,
For once, and found himself half-running
    To drop some for a jug of wine,

Perhaps a plate of smoking meat.
Anything left he wouldn't bleat
    At home, but stash for a sadder time.

The strong greaved arm that jerked him out
From the mob, on the beaten route
    Toward Skull Hill, seemed to come from nowhere.

So did the voice that broke his ear,
And the bruised man they pushed him near,
    And that blunt wood which he must now bear.

He tried to smile at the crowd staring,
As if it were a joke, this sharing
    At some hired foreign thug's command,

A carpenter's toy of nail and limb.
A mule-faced boy laughed on with him.
    But then the wood's edge cut his hand,

His purse split wide beneath its weight
And coins gushed, trailing them through the gate.
    He felt a whip when he tried to turn.

"Where is your kingdom and your glory?"
He heard, and thought, "Not me. This sorry
    Slave who's been cast out and will burn."

VI. Veronica Wipes the Face of Jesus

He stopped a moment, when her eyes
Met his and grieved to recognize
   The mark of suffering in his face.

With a slow hand, she drew her veil,
Revealed herself, ashamed and pale,
   As if awaiting his embrace.

But he stood, stultified, eyes bloodshot.
She wiped his face, although that could not
   Stitch his ripped brow or salve his pains.

Standing back, then, as the crowd throbbed,
She saw the white square had been daubed
   With the grave portrait of his looks,

As if to prove, in every prayer
Our airy words melt at his stare;
   And even his words, in our books,

Are nothing to the fact of flesh,
The staining of the thorn-pricked mesh
   Upon a piece of woven cloth.

Think of Bouguereau's painted saints,
Their aureoles like pewter plates
   To show the heft of spirit's troth;

For our ideas are fading things,
Wants change with what the weather brings,
   But this stamped weight of being remains.

VII. Jesus Falls the Second Time

All gold leaves to the earth returning,
The hungry winds cracked panes discerning,
  To shriek and scour the season's dark.

This child lifts his knee newly bloodied;
And that stares down at iced cake muddied,
  Dropped during her birthday in the park.

Spinner seeds, spiders, Throne and Power,
The divorcee curled in the shower,
  As the steam rises over her groan.

All bombs, balloons, and shining gold hair,
The patient's jaw when the scan showed there
  Malignant cells or waking life.

To see by chance a line of Scripture,
Or mispronounce it; the discomfiture
  Of witches' spells; or the thief's knife

Raised before eyes naïve to fate.
Yet, you lay, pure beneath your weight,
  These things to you already known.

VIII. Jesus Speaks to the Women of Jerusalem

He turned to those who stood in tears
As if to coax away their fears
   With promises of his bright kingdom.

But here is what he actually said:
"A day will come, when, sons unbred,
   Bare wombs, stripped bodies feel like treasure;

A day enthralled to vivid fictions,
Benumbed on doctors' strong prescriptions,
   And docile at the expert's measure.

A day when men, at last, will cease
To take my fearsome kiss of peace,
   But covet every moment's pleasure."

They watched him turn to climb the hill,
His flesh dragged by a hidden will,
   And wondered what his death would bring them.

IX. Jesus Falls a Third Time

The first fall, they say, quickly flashed,
As Lucifer saw his light surpassed
   And fired the hosts with his brash call.

We think the second came in Eden,
When curious thought like fruit was eaten,
   Digesting paradise to dust.

The third one is less sure. When *was* it?
The Flood, Exile, David in his closet,
   Drawing Bathsheba to his lust?

To nail a moment to its message
Is hard for us. What does it presage?
   It may not mean a thing at all.

Three times Aeneas' arms clutch the air
Intent to find his father there,
   But gather nothing to his chest.

Three times a voice disturbs your dreams
Before you guess it's what it seems.
   To bear news of a curse you're blessed.

Three times Christ asked him, "Do you love me?"
How many times must he absolve me
   Till I grasp who's saved by his fall?

X. Jesus Is Stripped of His Garments

The day they rushed him in the street,
His buck-toothed face flushed like a beet,
   One stomped his calves and watched him drop.

Another, with a dry limb snapped
Off the sick apple tree, then rapped
   Him on his ribs and wouldn't stop.

From then on, he was called the Mule.
Just so, this woman at the pool,
   Slipping thick legs and small breasts in,

Overhears the eddies of contempt.
And the old pervert, when he's sent
   To prison, lives with threats, and then,

Chokes on blood while the guard's at lunch.
So, though they'd whip and crown and punch
   You, till your robe was sopping red,

They stripped it off and pierced your side,
Leaving you nothing left to hide,
   There stretched out on the wooden bed.

XI. Jesus is Nailed to the Cross

For boys who pull the wings off beetles
Or prick their sisters' backs with needles,
   They spread his hand to take the nail.

For we who meet in dark motels
To clasp a stranger to ourselves,
   His palm split as they drove the nail.

You, the one who frisked through her purse,
When she stepped out to find the nurse,
   For you they placed a second nail.

While I got drunk this afternoon,
A child's skull was torn from the womb,
   Its cries rung in the hammered nail.

This whole world is a pile of skulls.
We like it so, lest our sense dulls.
   Watch them brace his feet for the nail!

For us, who keep our kitchens clean,
Who'd never have ourselves thought mean,
   We had them drive the final nail,

And set him hanging, his fists bleeding,
While we went shopping, preening, feeding,
   And in his shadow pared our nail.

XII. Jesus Dies on the Cross

His limbs splayed, writhing, as he hung there,
Murmuring of a kingdom somewhere
   The Roman guards had never been.

The sun beat on his darkened head.
He barely heard what the good thief said,
   So swollen and plugged his ears were then.

"I thirst," his mother heard him cry.
"Why have you left me here to die?"
   But then, more placid, "Here's your son."

He said that, looked from her to John,
Till they saw what was going on,
   And all at once clouds hid the sun.

XIII. Jesus is Taken Down from the Cross

This morning, I hauled to the street
A heavy wooden pallet so beat
    The workmen had left it behind.

Its boards, rough-hewn and splintering
Along the stone, I let it lean
    Against the dumpster, with some twined

And flattened cardboard boxes, too.
A March gust puffed its chest and blew
    To overturn what I had built.

The hard wood clattered on the road
And split, exposed its secret load
    Of bent and rusted nails, now spilt,

Scattered like seeds, like teeth and bones,
Awaiting tires, the feet of Jones
    Too lost in song to watch his step.

One nail stared up from the cracked wood.
I plucked it out, just as they would
    Who returned you to your mother's lap.

XIV. Jesus Is Laid in the Tomb

They thought of Saul fallen on his sword,
Of Jonah swallowed with his word,
 Of John's head staring from its platter,

As they set his upon the stone.
One said, "If he's God's chosen one,
 What they have done to him won't matter."

"Yes," said another, "Lazarus
Is fine, and death's unreal for us."
 Agreed, they lingered at the door.

"But something in me finds it awful,
The way they beat him." "Was it lawful,
 To watch? Or should we have done more?"

Burnt umber stained the linen cloth
Wrapped over face and hands. A moth
 Made of his side a moment's bed.

And all the sounds of evening pressed
Upon their silence without rest.
 "The women will anoint his head."

"Perhaps they'll let us pray outside."
As each one spoke, he felt he'd lied,
 As if there were something understood

They would have said, but could not speak,
That didn't feign strength when they were weak,
 Whose glory lay in stiffened blood.

VI

A man does not join himself with the Universe so long
as he has anything else to join himself with

∽T. S. Eliot

IN THE VILLAGE OF BERWYN

My hands throb, cracked and ruddy with the winter.
Along the back fence, deer have crept at night
To strip our evergreens to their last splinter,
Until my futile bark sets them in flight,
    Their bright legs fading through the neighboring park.
    I turn, and shut the door against the dark.

The hallway boards are whited, smeared with salt.
Puffed boots, kicked off, lie soaking with wet socks.
The children whisper, shift in bed, then halt,
Halt at the slow creak as their father walks.
    They listen, and I hear them listen there,
    For where I go, for what my hands may bear.

How Many Exiles in the Monastery

How many exiles in the monastery
   Copied some painted page in heavy tomes
And filled its margins with the spry but weary
   Details recalled of their forsaken homes?

Some displaced readers down the centuries
   Have opened Dante's *De vulgari* and found
Their pains ginned up as pride's rhetorical breeze:
   Pure language is the great man's native ground.

When, over cheap newspaper blurbs, we see
   A plane's white snout shredding the parceled sky—
A discount angel's posed sublimity
   That loathes outmoded bones—we know its lie:

The placeless freedom some words have is not
Ours; they're what's left when our homes go to rot.

EPITHALAMIUM

October 20, 2007

Dear Lynn, I haven't met you yet, and yet,
    Because of your groom's frank and free oblations
    In sonnet sequences or while we drink,
In permanent print or on the internet,
    I write to share my cheerful approbations
    For what I cannot know but may still think.
An age like ours forbids discourse on taste,
    Either because it "don't" sound democratic,
    Or just because the sheer "ubiquitousness"
Of violence and vulgarity has laid waste
    To standards; we stow our judgments in the attic.
    But please indulge me. Let me tell you this, Miss:
If Ernie's store of trivia, wit, and words is full,
    As Plato says, it still took you to make him whole.

Laundry and James Tate

Shortly before I moved from Amherst, Mass.
A famous poet friend of mine walked past,
His laundry bag slung over withered shoulders,
Worn out with writing poems about ham,
Boobies of many hues, the Son of Sam.

I had been idling at the Laundromat
Myself, and soon would dry my soiled load
Of knee socks till they fit like normal socks.
In youth, he'd joined a secret commune vowing
Never to wash his own, he let me know.

"And that shop there will do it cheap." He told
Me also, there were others growing old
And stubborn on their way to leave their socks
In the steam-wrinkled hands of Chinese women.
I told him back, I wished I hadn't heard.

Or rather, wished he would have said as much
A long, long time before. What good it do
Me now? My final load of shirts and socks
Shrinking behind me while I shot the shit?
The towns that light the winter darkness in

New England's Presbyterian western woods
Are full of secret pacts I'll never learn
Of, full of old men whispering of whites
And darks in places where Ben Franklin stood.
They meditate upon his list of virtues—

Not the one we all know about. Another.
They trace their ancestries of cryptic blood.
They put together puzzles of mad snakes.
And in their temples mumble through old rites.
You never know who is or not a brother.

"Thanks anyway, Jim," I said, and turned forever
From wealthy Masonries I could not join,
Naively trusting to the drier's eye
In whose abyss my socks were spinning stars
To light a pilgrim's way beyond the Berkshires.

ECCE HOMO

I have started asking for power.
My friends mostly.
I would like power of attorney
Or to be charged with feeding their golden retriever
While they are in Florida on vacation.

The two of them go there every year now.

I see them running on a beach.
Or sitting on blankets, reading.

When I picture the bronze-age fleece
Of his chest, burnished in cocoa oil
The picture blots out

And I go back to thinking about me.

I've never been.
When they get back, I certainly don't ask to see any pictures.

She just smiles while her husband writes out the check in the kitchen.

Her glossy lips beam.
She's squatted down, flexed legs tightly balanced,
In dark hose and the gray skirt she wears for air travel.

Her free hand is buried
In the shaggy, thick flank of the dog
Who's already gone back to sleep.

That's when I start to crave additional power.

And I see gulls begin to rise before me as I run,

Run through the splashing littoral,
The dog's mane matted and salty at my side.

That is the only world there ever was for me.

AFTER THE ASCENSION

Ascension Thursday's gone again,
   And leaves an idle sorrow here
That settles on the heart and brain.
I'd hoped to renew everything,
   To feel, for good, grace sitting near,
Crowned with the glory of the spring.

But, no, a restlessness instead,
   One like a crow's beak at my breast,
Whose only seed is sin and dread.
As if my only speech were sighs,
   And only violence could impress
Itself on dulled, rapacious eyes.

The light goes up and leaves a shroud.
   We savored an extended feast
As he broke bread, ate, and allowed
Our fingers to press in each wound.
   Now, though from every bond released,
We're left staring on a hollow mound.

Some Will Remember You

The work of salvation takes place in obscurity and
stillness. In the heart's quiet dialogue with God the
living building blocks out of which the kingdom of
God grows are prepared, the chosen instruments for
the construction forged.

~ St. Teresa Benedicta of the Cross

I

Some will remember you for what they call you,
A curious fact or novelty, and some will
Remember chiefly how you died, and linger
On blood's enthralling stain. Still others may
Enter within your final silence, find
The life that did not know it begged salvation,
But the mere clarity of things and thought;
The one who chattered in the corridors
Of Being, took tea with Husserl, before
The interior mountain beckoned you to climb,
The floors of the self-darkened room first creaked.
You wrote out what you saw and then sought stillness.
And not for what you said but what you were,
Not for your truest name, you were packed off
To death. After the smoke, bones left forgotten,
Your jotted notes shut in a metal trunk,
As others bore reprisals and arrests,
Your thought lived in the study of a priest.

II

In evil times and aftertimes, in times
When all the stubbled fields of action smolder,
Bowed heads can't help but make their patient study
Of how the person worlds. In his wired room—
With worship driven back through unmarked doors,
And the earth gutted by the tread of foreign
Tanks—he would read your half-lost books, would speak
Their words into the empty air for all
The stashed and sensitive microphones to hear.

In those times, your words, carried on the quiet,
Fostered his own. Thought, act, and judging person,
The self in solitude revealing God,
Clicked like the murdered signal of your voice
Across a telegraph and moved his hand.
Below the frequencies of the State radio,
That remnant bookish beauty leaned into
His ear: a ghostly Carmelite with time
Enough to stipple out accented thoughts
On where our thinking natures drive themselves.

While you were still a student, restless, hard,
Unchained still from the science of the cross,
Too lost in thought to think a knock could come,
The brown shirts there to haul your body off
Beyond its cloistral habit, even then
Your tattered typescripts sealed within themselves
A whole new vision of our thinking, living,
Our radiant way of knowing through our seeing.
And these, in time, would fill Wojtyła's head,
Though you'd have long mixed ashes with the dead.

III
What terrible love did she bear
The soldiers massed about the steeple,
Breaking the sisters from their prayer?
"Come, we are going for our people."

Pressed in the rattling cattle car
Between her sister and rough board,
Drawn through the final smoke of war?
"Come, we are going to our Lord."

IV
This life: she'd graphed its pattern on the page,
The frail inconstant forms of bone and speech,
And gave to one mind, tranquil in an age
Of violence, wisdom which no war could reach.
Not in her name as Jew or Carmelite;

Not just in death, her study's parasite;
But in the working out of truth and choice,
In words that prayed when others lapsed to rage,
She'd guide, perhaps, the bullet, guide the voice
Of John Paul up the mountain of an age.

V

Those years after,
The Successor
From his throne,
Voice hoarse, intoned
That she was neither
Casualty nor teacher,
But philosopher
And holy martyr,
Jewish daughter,
Church's doctor,
Spiritual mother,
Illumined voice
Of reason and choice,
A converted heart
Who'd played her part,
A sainted sign
Named Edith Stein.

ON THIS RICH GROUND

For the Wedding of JL and DP
September 21, 2013

On this rich ground
Where the vines promise
To visit upon us
Fruit for wine presses,
We gather round,
In decorous colors,
In coats and collars
And formal dresses.

We stand upright
And speak such word
As may be heard
In fitting measure.
For, though at night,
Wild thoughts in the deep
Unravel our sleep,
These bring no pleasure.

It pleases, rather,
In wakefulness
To praise and bless
What grows and gives
To thoughtless matter
Its purposes.
As Genesis says
All that lives

Fulfills itself
In those who turn
To another and learn
To live as one,
Self given to self,
Voice answering voice.
So we rejoice
To see this done,

To witness this day
Take on new meaning
In the convening
Of two who love.
Though words pass away
Like autumn weather,
They bind forever
What's below and above.

AUTUMN ROAD

I follow the clean-edged macadam north
To catch the train, the maples hanging forth
On either side, their leaves of brilliant reds,
Oranges, and umbers that will make their beds
Soon in the unmown grass that lines my street,
And crumble at the weight of passing feet.
    The people who just moved in three doors down
Have ringed their banisters in black and brown
And hung a skeletal child from a swing,
Its eyeless stare a dark and menacing
Reminder to pray for the dead and of those
Horrors the coming darkness may disclose.
We haven't met the tenants yet, and don't
Want to. A glance into their yard has sown
Nightmares already in my children's sleep,
Shaking them teared and screaming from its deep.
We've heard them crush their beer cans, out to smoke
Late at night, and guffaw at some crude joke.
A few doors farther on, the lawn is spiked
With signs for candidates I've long disliked.
Just seeing their names induces in me fear
Less supernatural but much more near
At hand than those that haunt the children's dreams.
    But then, I see that stone foundations, beams
Of smooth pine pitched high in the sun, where two
Homes now are rising, promise something new;
And hear St. Monica's bell in her tower
Govern our hillside as it tolls the hour,
Chastening us that though our time seems dire,
Much has endured through beating rains and fire,
And good can still be made in this dark season.
    I read a book last week that says our reason
No longer sees the world as from God's eyes;
Where the ancient mind saw signs, ours now denies
To it all but the most material meaning.
    I'm not so sure. It seems that thoughts are leaning
Up against every fence post, and the earth,
Stared at, stares back and quietly brings to birth
Between us morals, words, and promises

Which we might overlook but can't dismiss.
I worry, as a father, that the year
Ahead will bear out omens all too clear
Such that my children, grown, will only know
The clash of good and evil's fiery glow.
    I stop to let the speeding traffic pass.
The gutter's tiled with tins and broken glass.
Across the way, the Veteran's Memorial
With polished granite, stirring flags, and aureole
Of silver guards the entrance to the station.
Its plaque says, *These gave their lives for our nation.*
I wait, clutching my ticket in my hand,
For what the rough voiced future will demand.

ACKNOWLEDGMENTS

All of these poems first appeared in various journals and magazines, sometimes under different titles and almost always in very different forms. The author thanks the editors of the following magazines for their counsel and encouragement.

Seven poems from "The Stations of the Cross" first appeared in different magazines: "I. Jesus Is Condemned" and "IV. Jesus Meets His Mother," in *The San Diego Reader*; "VI. Veronica Wipes the Face of Jesus," "XI. Jesus Is Nailed to the Cross," and "XII. Jesus Dies on the Cross," in *First Things*; "XIII. Jesus Is Taken Down from the Cross," in *America*; and "XIV. Jesus Is Laid in the Tomb," in *Dappled Things*. All fourteen poems were subsequently published as a series, with illustrations by Daniel Mitsui, in *The Clarion Review*.

The poems in "The Mountains of China" and "*Ecce Homo*" first appeared in *The Bend*; "To Ernest Hilbert" in *Literary Matters*; "Some Will Remember You" and "The Consolation of Oranges," in *Dappled Things*; "After the Ascension," "Epithalamium," and "Autumn Road," in *First Things*; all the sonnets of "Wiped Out" and "Dreams that Come Friday" appeared in *The Raintown Review*; "Reckonings" in *Chronicles*; "In the Village of Berwyn," "See," "Bright Apples," and "The Book of Kings," in *Measure*; "During the Protests" and "The Recluse," in *Humanitas*; "Passover," in *The New Criterion*; "Laundry and James Tate," in *Light*; "In Sickness," in *The Evansville Review*; "On this Rich Ground" and "Histories," in *Modern Age*; and "The Scar of Odysseus" and "How Many Exiles in the Monasteries," in *Alabama Literary Review*.

About the Author

James Matthew Wilson is the author of seven previous books, including *The Vision of the Soul: Truth, Goodness, and Beauty in the Western Tradition* (Catholic University of America Press, 2017), *The Fortunes of Poetry in an Age of Unmaking* (Wiseblood, 2015), *Some Permanent Things* (Wiseblood, 2014), *The Catholic Imagination in Modern American Poetry* (Wiseblood, 2014), *The Violent and the Fallen* (Finishing Line Press, 2013), *Timothy Steele: A Critical Introduction* (Story Line Press, 2012), and *Four Verse Letters* (Steubenville, 2010). The 2017 winner of the Hiett Prize from the Dallas Institute of Humanities and Culture, he is Associate Professor of Humanities and Augustinian Traditions at Villanova University, and Poetry Editor of *Modern Age* magazine. He lives in the village of Berwyn, Pennsylvania, with his wife and children.